This Book Belongs To

_____

Dedication:

This book is dedicated to all the mermaid lovers out there, who find wonder and magic beneath the sea. May the beautiful merfolk, sirens, and aquatic creatures of our Mermaid coloring book transport you to a realm of enchantment and relaxation.

Thank you for choosing our book and for allowing us to be a part of your mermaid journey.

Happy Coloring!

BONUS: Get 10 Free Printable Coloring Pages!

Get 10 free, printable illustrations! Use your smartphone camera on the QR code to visit us in your mobile browser!

REIGN OF READS

She dances with the waves
and dreams with the sea.

Please use the section below to test your coloring tools. Press as hard as you would normally. If you feel the need use a separate piece of paper or a spacer under each coloring sheet.

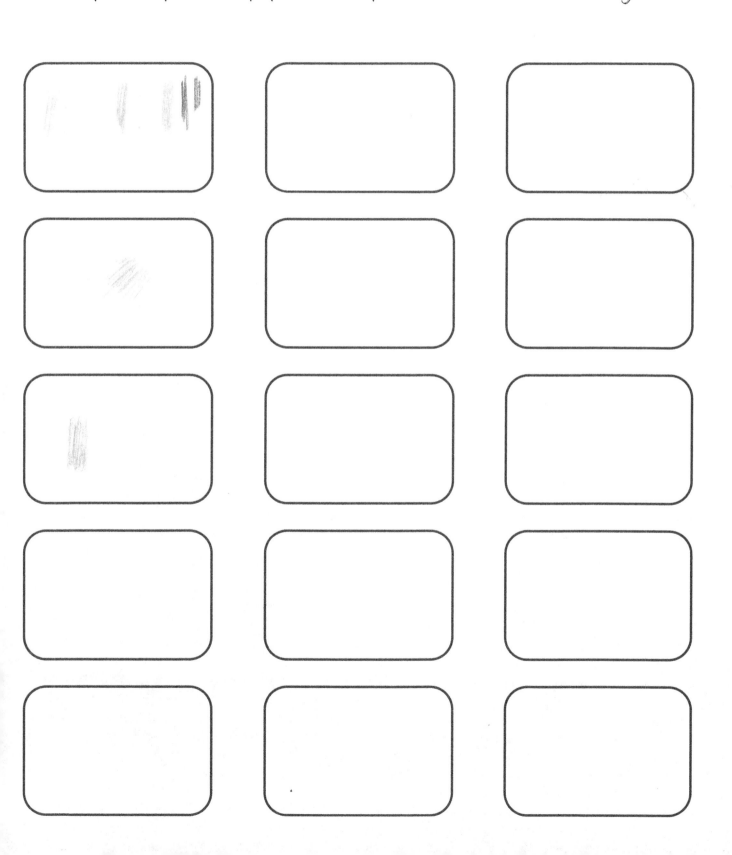

In a sea of ordinary,
be a mermaid.

Let the currents guide

your dreams.

Believe in magic, believe in yourself
—be a mermaid.

Embrace your inner mermaid
and let your spirit soar.

Mermaids don't drown
in water; they are
born to swim.

Make waves with your dreams
and let them carry you.

The ocean calls and
the mermaid follows.

Be a mermaid who
creates her own waves.

Life is better under the sea,
where dreams become reality.

Let the magic of the sea
ignite your soul.

Discover the treasures within,
like a hidden mermaid.

Like a mermaid, dive into the depths of your desires.

Mermaids know the
secrets of the tides.

In a world of fish,

be a mermaid.

Follow your heart's compass,
just like a wandering mermaid.

Be a mermaid and make

waves of happiness.

Mermaids collect moments,

not things.

Dive deep, explore, and
let your spirit splash.

The ocean is full of wonders,
just like the heart of a mermaid.

Mermaids have the courage to
dive into the unknown..

She is like the sea:
fierce, beautiful, and free.

Embrace your uniqueness,

just like a mermaid

in a sea of fish.

Life's a beach—find your inner mermaid and enjoy the waves.

Beach hair, don't care—
mermaid life is all
about the freedom.

Every day is a chance to
swim into your dreams.

In a world full of reality,
dare to be a mermaid.

She was a mermaid who danced with
the waves and chased the sunsets.

Mermaids dream in shades of turquoise and aquamarine.

Be a mermaid and leave a little sparkle wherever you go.

Like a mermaid, let the depths
of your soul shine through.

Mermaids find their power in the ebb and flow of the ocean.

Follow the call of the sea and let it lead you to your destiny.

Dive into the adventure and swim fearlessly, just like a mermaid.

She was like a mermaid, captivating hearts with her grace and beauty.

Mermaids don't wait for the storm to pass; they learn to dance in the waves.

She was a mermaid who longed for the stars and found them in her dreams.

Be a mermaid and let the waves
carry you to new horizons.

Find your own rhythm, like a
mermaid swimming through the tides.

Believe in magic, for mermaids are proof that dreams come true.

Be fierce and fearless, just like a mermaid in the deep blue sea.

Mermaids enchant with their beauty and inspire with their courage.

The ocean is a treasure trove of dreams,
waiting to be explored by mermaids.

Let your imagination swim with the mermaids and create your own fairy tales beneath the waves.

Mermaids remind us to dive into life with wonder and curiosity.

Be a mermaid who leaves a trail
of magic wherever she goes.

Like a mermaid, let the waves
wash away your worries
and bring you serenity.

Mermaids believe in the beauty of their dreams and the power of their hearts.

Embrace the depths of your soul, for there lies the essence of a mermaid.

Mermaids inspire us to embrace our true selves and swim against the currents.

Dream big, swim deep, and let your inner mermaid shine.

In a world of ordinary, be the extraordinary mermaid that makes waves.